THE FAITHFUL FAMILIES TOOLKIT

Traci Smith

For more information about Family Faith Every Day,
visit www.familyfaitheveryday.com

Cover design and interior illustrations: Paul Soupiset www.paulsoupiset.com

Interior design: Connie H. C. Wang

ISBN 9780827211612

ChalicePress.com

Table of Contents

Welcome

Welcome to the *Faithful Families Toolkit*! In picking this workbook up and deciding to embark on the journey within, you've done one of the hardest parts already. You've decided to dedicate yourself to learning how to incorporate faith practices in your daily life to grow closer to God and your family! Over the next eight sessions, you'll start putting tools in your kit to help you on this journey.

These sessions were designed using the research and feedback of over a decade's worth of conversations and small groups just like yours. Since 2014, I've heard from hundreds of families who have tried some of the practices in this book. They've told me what works, what doesn't, and what they wish they knew before they got started. I've compiled all this knowledge into the workbook you have before you.

As you embark on this journey, I pray that you may rest in the knowledge that God goes with you. One of the shiniest verses of Scripture in my view is this one: "Ask, and it will be given to you; search, and you will find; knock, and the door will be opened for you. For everyone who asks receives, and everyone who searches finds, and for everyone who knocks, the door will be opened.[1]" I trust that as you work your way through these sessions you will notice the Spirit of Christ with you every step of the way. Enjoy the journey. It is here for you.

Traci Smith, 2024.

[1] Matthew 7:7-8 NRSV

About This Workbook

There are two main components to this workbook that, together, make up the *Faithful Families* system of learning faith habits at home:

1. The first component includes the lessons you will complete with your groups over eight sessions. Your group leader will provide directions around how often, when, and where your group meets. Some groups will meet monthly, others weekly, and still others on a different schedule. You'll notice as you flip through the lessons that each lesson is designed with a similar structure. After a time of check-in and prayer, you'll share stories together that draw you into the topic and theme for the week. You'll then reflect on a Scripture together, also on this same theme. After your group reflection, you'll have time to work on an individual worksheet or journaling exercise before you come back together for further learning and discussion. At the end of the lesson time, you'll close as you began—by sharing joys and concerns and adjourning with prayer.
2. The second component includes the faith practices you will complete as a family each week. You can think of this as your "homework." This system is about helping you establish faith habits at home that will last for many years to come, and it's essential that you start practicing the faith habits right away—both to start forming the habit and to contribute to the group discussion in the following weeks. The practices are found in the companion book *Faithful Families: Creating Sacred Moments at Home*. Before beginning, you should review the book and the practices, so you are familiar with the various faith practices and their instructions. Each week, after you complete a faith practice, you'll record your experience in the faith practices journal section of your workbook, beginning on p. 71. This record will help you establish that faith habit, help you identify what is working for your family, and help you make adjustments that lead to a more fulfilling and effective faith practice. At the conclusion of the lesson, some families may choose to continue

recording feedback on their faith habits and others may decide to continue with the faith practice without logging it. Though the system may seem overly regimented, I've found the structure to be necessary and helpful to achieving the goal of consistent faith practice at home.

About the Author

Hi! I'm Traci Smith, the author of the *Faithful Families* series of books as well as this companion toolkit. I'm an ordained Presbyterian Minister and (together with my husband, Rev. Elias Cabarcas) the mother of three children. My passion is helping families find connection and meaning through faith practice.

I began this journey in 2014 with the publication of *Faithful Families: Creating Sacred Moments at Home* (then published under a different name). In the decade-plus that followed the publication of *Faithful Families,* I've talked to dozens of families who have used the book and heard from hundreds more. The feedback has been consistent: families like the practices, but they often find it challenging to remember to do them, to keep them in front of their families, and to be transformed by them.

In talking with faith formation leaders and families about what *does* work and in training families to use the practices to create faith habits, I designed this workbook. It represents my decade-long experience with and my best instincts about forming faith habits at home. I look forward to hearing your experiences with this material to continue to create new and better resources for you!

About Family Faith Every Day

Family Faith Every Day is a program of Chalice Media Group, a leading publisher in the progressive Christian marketplace and the publishing house of the Christian Church (Disciples of Christ) for more than a century.

Family Faith Every Day is made possible in part by a grant from Lilly Endowment Inc.'s Christian Parenting and Caregiving Initiative. Created in 2023, the initiative helps parents and caregivers pass on the faith to their children. This generous support allows Family Faith Every Day to thoroughly research the ideas Traci Smith, and the *Faithful Families* series has been road-testing for a decade as she's put our bestselling *Faithful Families* books out into the world. This support also creates the opportunity to work directly with congregations and Christian educators and provide direct support.

Family Faith Every Day Has Four Priorities

- Publish resources that help families practice faith-at-home.
- Support congregations as they teach families how to practice faith-at-home.
- Research the effectiveness of faith-at-home practices and share our findings with congregations and parents.
- Provide continuing education opportunities for faith formation leaders and pastors around faith-at-home practices.

As groups around the country follow along with this workbook (our very first resource published under the Family Faith Every Day Program!) and work through the lessons, some participants will be opting into a research component where we'll be able to study what they've learned and make suggestions that will allow the workbook to continue to morph and change. To all the churches that are embarking on this journey knowing that you are a part of this valuable research: thank you! You are helping thousands of families grow closer to God and one another. To keep up with our ongoing efforts and research please visit www.familyfaitheveryday.com

FAITHFUL FAMILIES' PHILOSOPHY IS:

Simple, but Not Easy

Like many things worth doing in life, establishing faith habits as a family takes effort. One of the things we've found useful is to be realistic about the effort required to make lasting and effective change. The faith practices we suggest are simple and take little time to complete. Nearly all of them take less than fifteen minutes, and most take less than five. You can do them with little or no preparation, and they don't take a lot of background knowledge or theological training to understand. All that said, it's not always easy to establish new habits and keep at it through the challenges life throws at us. These sessions will help you see what some of the challenges might be and give you time and space to work through them.

A System/Way of Living

The *Faithful Families* books and toolkit take you through simple practices to do at home to grow closer to God and one another. Undergirding these practices is the belief that faith is learned as it is woven seamlessly through the fabric of everyday life.[2] Rather than focusing on perfection in the practices, focus on what they achieve in aggregate over a lifetime of practicing them. Our hope is that the *Faithful Families* system isn't just a passing fad, but that it's something you allow to burrow deep within your family's core values and way of living. Like a recipe book, *Faithful Families* is intended to teach you a few favorites you will adjust, change, and make your own. If you discover a new practice or make your own... great! Every family will find what works for them. Over the next eight sessions, you'll have the opportunity to share what you're learning with other families and see it in practice. After this length of time, you'll have enough of a foundation to give it a try; but don't

[2] Please see the Introduction of *Faithful Families: Creating Sacred Moments* at Home, beginning on page 1.

be discouraged if you need to return to this book repeatedly to remember the lessons and recommit yourself to the practice. We encourage you to keep up with Family Faith Every Day online as well, for additional tips, training materials, and help establishing your practice.[3]

Community-Oriented

Ask your peers how willing they are, on a scale of one to ten, to help you out if you need them. "Nine," they'll say. "Ten, even." If they're the kind of friends I have, they'll say "Eleven out of ten. I'm moving in." Most people enjoy being helpful and are ready to jump at the opportunity. How willing would you be to help if someone asked you? Now rate yourself on a scale of one to ten in terms of how willing you are to *ask* for help. That's a bit different, isn't it? Negative ten out of ten is most people's response. "I hate asking for help" is something I hear all the time from parents. The result is that everybody's walking around with a bunch of people all around who would jump at the chance to help them, but they never get to receive the help, because nobody ever asks. Session seven is devoted to this concept, but it's worth beginning this study with the idea of community in mind. Who is traveling this road with you? How can you support one another?

Good Enough

British pediatrician Donald Winnicott introduced the concept of the "good enough mother" in 1953, explaining that minor failures in caregiving help children build emotional strength. Winnicott's conclusion was based on his observation of thousands of babies and their mothers.[4]

Mothers (and fathers) know we aren't perfect, but society seems to reinforce messages that we should be, or at least try to be. What would it look like if we, instead of aiming for perfection, aimed to be good enough? It's not that we don't strive for beautiful and excellent things, but it does mean we remind ourselves, repeatedly, that we can't be perfect. We must be good enough. In the same way, this

---

[3] www.familyfaitheveryday.com

[4] Winnicott, D. W.. *The Child, The Family, And The Outside World.* United Kingdom, Da Capo Press, 1987.

program is meant to be good enough. At the conclusion of your lessons, the hope is that you'll continue your faith practice, and we trust that many of you will. Even as you do, though, your practice will be imperfect. You'll stop and start. You'll pick it up, maybe after years of being away. If you forget to do a practice or lose your way, you'll come back. No guilt. No judgment. Good enough.

A Joy

My two oldest children, both boys, are nearly twelve months apart in age, and they spent a lot of time in a special double stroller together. They drew a lot of attention as loud babies do. Time and time again, folks would make the same comment: "You must have your hands full!" It was true, I did, but the comment always bothered me. I felt self-conscious. *Do the boys look disheveled*? I thought. *Do* I? If they didn't comment about me having my hands full, they asked if I was going to have a little girl one day, which I always thought was rude to them—and me. One day, a cashier in the grocery store started admiring the boys in their stroller in the same way "Wow! Two boys, so close together! You must..." I braced myself "Be very happy."

I still tear up thinking about that lovely comment. It was exactly right, and it was exactly what I wanted to hear as I strolled around the store with those two precious boys. "I know you are busy, and you probably have your hands full, but wow, aren't children an unbelievable blessing sometimes?" I hope you embark on this program with a sense of joy and delight. It's meant to be fun and meaningful for you. If this is a season of too much in terms of grief or health or life, don't "power through," just sit this one out and join a different time. It's meant to be a joy for you and your family and something to savor.

The Vital Role of Parents and Caregivers in Faith Formation at Home

In their book *Handing Down the Faith* professors Christian Smith and Amy Adamczyk offer a comprehensive analysis of how children learn faith at home. In their introduction they summarize dozens of studies that talk about the nuances in terms of how children learn faith at home. I commend the entire book to anyone who is interested in getting deep into the nitty gritty of this topic. One overarching thing to know, however, is this: parents are the number one influence on a child's faith development. The role of the congregation is to support what is taught and led at home. It's simply insufficient to count on faith being learned through church attendance alone. Perhaps this truth is scary or challenging for you. Perhaps it's liberating and exciting. Maybe it's both. As you work through these lessons know this: though your role is essential, you are not without support and resources. Your peers are on this journey with you, and your congregation is here to support you. If you found your way to this resource, you've already overcome a major hurdle.

Before You Begin: Practical Tips

Commit to the Time for the Lessons and the Practices: One of the things I *want* to say (and your leader does, too) is that "life is busy and it's okay to just come when you can. Don't worry about it." However, when something is important, it's a priority. These lessons are designed to go together, like interlocking pieces of a puzzle, and they're designed for impact. Both the lessons and the faith practices you do at home can have a profound effect on your family's faith if you commit to it. So as much as I want to say, "Just come when you can," the better message is, "Do everything you can to prioritize this group for the next eight sessions."

In creating the curriculum, we've worked hard to make sure that all the lessons are essential and meaningful. The material has been tested and refined. With great commitment comes great results, and that's what you can expect from these next eight weeks.

Be Flexible: This is the flip side of commitment. Life is unpredictable, and if you must miss a session or a practice, have grace with yourself! Perhaps you can make up the material one on one with your leader or get together over coffee with one of your group members.

Review the Structure of the Workbook, the Storytelling Questions and the Practices in *Faithful Families*: As explained previously, the toolkit is designed as a companion to the book *Faithful Families: Creating Sacred Moments at Home*. Review the book carefully before you begin. It's a lot like a recipe book in that you don't need to read it cover to cover. Skim through and get oriented to which practices you might like to try. I also suggest reading through the lessons in this workbook, so you are familiar with what is planned. Resist the urge to "work ahead," however, as there's a special kind of magic in doing them in a group.

Set an Intention for the Time: What do you hope to gain in the eight sessions of this program? The hope is that you'll gain the tools you need to embark on a journey of practicing faith at home with your family for as long as your children are in your home with you (and even beyond). Is there something beyond this that's important to you? Perhaps you and your spouse could use some extra time together in connection or conversation and you'll take some extra time before or after the gatherings for dinner or dessert. Perhaps you want to take advantage of the family faith practice time around an area of your routine that's already a challenge, such as mealtime or bedtime. What would make the time most successful for you?

Notes for Group Leaders

When putting a group together that will meet several times, attention to detail is key. This toolkit is designed for group use with the express goal that parents and caregivers will form a trusting relationship with one another throughout the eight sessions. As you put your group together, consider the following:

***When* will we meet?** This will be your biggest challenge, given the busy lives of families. The eight toolkit lessons are 90-minute sessions. This does not mean necessarily that the meetings must take place over eight consecutive weeks. For some, the lessons will need to be spread out over more than eight weeks to avoid holidays or church conflicts. Monthly meetings are also an option. For those who would like to do the lessons in a more concentrated format, all eight sessions could be incorporated into a retreat. Keep in mind that if you choose the retreat option, participants will not have had time between lessons to practice their faith-at-home homework with their families. This can still be accomplished after the conclusion of the retreat but will require follow up.

***Where* will we meet?** When our world shut down during the COVID-19 pandemic, everyone learned how to meet online. We learned a great deal about how to create community at a distance, and these lessons were valuable. That said, I strongly encourage in-person meetings for this curriculum. There is something very important about the energy shared in person and the fellowship that can take place in the presence of others. Take time and energy to think about the layout of the room, the comfort of the seating, and the softness of the lighting. A homey "living room" type of atmosphere mirrors a home environment and invites relaxed conversation.

***Who* should be invited to the group?** I encourage you to form a group of 5-8 parents/caregivers with at least 3 families represented in the group. Any smaller, and your group risks being awkwardly small. Any larger, and the group might not have time for in-depth discussion. In order to preserve community and keep everyone on the same page, I encourage you to avoid adding new participants once you've started. Many churches will need to offer multiple sessions of this curriculum or have "groups within the group" in order to accommodate everyone. Consider forming groups of parents with children of similar ages and stages.

***How* will we make the meeting attractive?** Meeting over a meal, snacks, or dessert takes extra effort but helps create community and an element of warmth.

***How* long will our meeting be?** I've budgeted approximate times for each section below. If you add a few minutes at the beginning and end of the meeting for gathering and dismissal, your group should fit comfortably into a 90-minute time slot. I caution you against trying to cram this meeting into 60 minutes, but if you must, consider taking two sessions per lesson. Moving through the material more slowly is preferable over racing through it.

In addition to the logistical details above, please familiarize yourself with the flow of the lessons and meetings before you begin. Understand the intention behind each part of the group gathering as laid out here. Using the routine of these lessons is key to their success! You are encouraged to adapt the routine for your congregation's context if needed. The meetings are designed to maintain a sense of rhythm and cohesion throughout the eight sessions to provide structure, clarity, and peace, and each element has been thoughtfully chosen.

ELEMENTS OF EACH LESSON

The Symbol

Time Commitment: 1-2 minutes at the beginning of each session.

Each lesson has a corresponding symbol that serves as a metaphor for what the lesson is about. Each symbol is listed in the table of contents and depicted both on the front cover and at the beginning of each lesson. Have fun with these symbols and refer to them throughout the lesson. Incorporate the symbols in your promotion of the class and follow up.

60-Second Update

Time Commitment: 5-10 minutes, depending on the size of your group.

Whether it's family life, professional life, or personal concerns, we come to a group experience like this with a lot on our minds beyond the study itself. It's helpful to give folks a chance to name what's on their minds without taking up too much time. Furthermore, it's important to allow equal "airtime" to each person as they give their update. For this reason, we suggest a very structured 60-second update time at the beginning of the lesson. The leader will set a timer for each person to give their update, gently reminding that the chime indicates it's time to move on to the next person. Over the course of the eight sessions, participants will develop a sense of how long a 60-second update is and may not need the timer anymore. Though it may feel awkward, hold yourself accountable to actually timing people and keeping them on track for this update. It will allow everyone the chance to share while still getting to the rest of the materials.

Opening Candle Prayer

Time Commitment: 5 minutes

This candle uses a repeated liturgical element and a faith practice to open each lesson. Find a large, unscented candle to use throughout the entire eight weeks of the practice. Lighting a candle at the beginning sets the time apart as holy and shows, by example, what it means to have a repeated practice for centering and grounding.

Storytelling

Time Commitment: 15-20 minutes

This is an essential piece of the group flow and process. Understanding how storytelling works in these lessons requires a bit more explanation than the other sections.

At the beginning of each lesson, you'll notice a prompt that says, "Tell a story about..." This storytelling section can be one of the most profound and meaningful parts of the lessons, but not without preparation and intention. Without preparation and intention, story time can get awkward! For this reason, we'll linger a little bit on the vision behind the storytelling moment and what it aims to accomplish.

Sharing and receiving stories can be a holy action. Author and teacher Mark Yaconelli lays out a guidebook for this in his beautiful book, *Between the Listening and the Telling: How Stories Can Save Us.* He writes, "We live in a world that is alive and generous and in need of care. Strangely, paradoxically, it is in serving and singing and telling our stories to one another that we discover the homecoming we've been longing for has been here, among and within us, along."[1] Storytelling is an art, and it's different than normal conversation. Yaconelli gives two simple rules for storytelling that can help guide the experience and make it more rewarding for all who participate.

1. **The storyteller should not be interrupted by anyone in the group when they're telling their story.** Yaconelli says that when people tell their stories, they are usually in a flow of how they want to say it and what they want to say. He says it's like a "trance." When someone interrupts with, "And how many people were in the car again?" Or "Is this your dad's mom or your mom's mom?" it interrupts that flow. Just listen to the story. When one storyteller is done, move on to the next.
2. **After the story is told, simply say, "Thank you"** and nothing else. So often when we hear stories, our tendency is to follow up, probe further, or even one up with our own thoughts or stories that the storyteller has inspired in us. When we do this, we sometimes dim the light of that person's story. So, for these eight weeks, when we tell stories, we'll let each one stand alone and without commentary. We'll practice hearing it and saying, "Thank you." Your facilitator will help keep you on track here and gently remind you if you interrupt or "tack on" to the stories.

---

[1] I heard these guidelines in an in person workshop given by Mr. Yaconelli at Elmhurst Presbyterian Church. Mark's book *Between the Listening and the Telling* provides a useful guide for storytelling.

By following these very simple guidelines for storytelling, I think you'll find that section of the group experience to be valuable and deeply meaningful. Since you have the prompts in your lessons, you can come prepared with which story you tell. Telling a vulnerable or challenging story can be hard, though the payoff is enormous.

Wisdom from Scripture

Time Commitment: 5 minutes

This is not formal or traditional Bible Study but, rather, a faith-at-home education course built on a biblical foundation. To further strengthen the study, faith formation leaders and pastors might consider preaching on these passages or studying them in greater depth before the beginning of these sessions or at their conclusion.

Reflective Activity

Time Commitment: 10 minutes

Each of the eight lessons has a small activity requiring a pen or pencil, the workbook, and individual reflection. Participants should work on these individually and then share their reflections with the wider group as they feel comfortable.

Group Questions

Time Commitment: 15-20 minutes

At this point in each lesson, participants will have had time to reflect individually, hear stories from one another, and ponder the wisdom from scripture. The questions are listed in order of importance, so don't worry if you don't get through all of them. Better to have a more in-depth conversation than to rush.

Closing Ritual and Prayer

Time Commitment: 5 minutes

The meeting ends with reflective silence and a few words spoken together. Blow out the candle to signify the end of the holy meeting time.

Building Faith Practice at Home

The "homework" for families is to begin building a faith practice at home through weekly practice. This is an *essential* part of this system. Encourage families to complete one of the practices as listed in the corresponding pages of the *Faithful Families* book and to fill out one of the journal pages beginning on page 71. As a leader it will be your responsibility to help families follow through on their faith practices at home, receive feedback on how they're going, and help them to establish solid habits. The goal of the *Faithful Families Toolkit* is to help families establish faith habits at home that last a lifetime! The purpose of the journal in the back is to hold families accountable to doing their homework. Feel free to treat it just like an encouraging teacher would and come around to put stickers or stamps on the pages! Make it fun, and send the message that the homework is required!

THE TOOLKIT

1. The Compass:
   Understanding Values

2. The Keys:
   Making a Commitment

3. The Clock:
   Finding Time

4. The Calendar:
   Establishing a Habit

5. The Camera:
   Enjoying Different Seasons

6. The Candle:
   Integrating Difficult Moments

7. The Postcard:
   Creating a Community

8. The Flashlight:
   Starting Before Ready

LESSON ONE

Understanding Values

Objective

Parents will be able to identify their most important values, and beliefs, as a guide for growing together with their children in faith as they practice at home.

The Symbol

Without a compass, adventurous hikers wander can aimlessly in the forest or on the mountain, and are easily lost. This simple tool helps orient us to where we're going. So, do our values. They guide and direct us to where we want our children to end up as we raise them in faith.

60-Second Update

Opening Candle Prayer

Leader: Thank you, God, for the gift of one another. Be near as we consider the values that are most important to us.

All: May the Spirit of Christ who lives within us, now move among us. Amen.

(light the candle)

Storytelling

Tell a story about a time when a parent, grandparent, or caregiver taught you something valuable by their *actions* (rather than their words).

Wisdom from Scripture

Micah 6:8 (NRSV): "He has told you, O mortal, what is good; and what does the LORD require of you but to do justice, and to love kindness, and to walk humbly with your God?"

Application of Scripture to Life

Micah's famous words clarify and provide purpose and direction. What does God require of God's people? Justice, kindness, and walking humbly with God. Simple, but not easy. Clear, but challenging. When you imagine your children leaving home one day, which values do you hope they carry with them? Which values are the most important to you and your family? Without this clarity, you might find it hard to embark on a journey of faith at home with your family because there will be a lack of clarity to guide your steps.

The philosopher Seneca said it this way: "If a man knows not to which port he sails, no wind is favorable." Taking a moment to reflect on where you're headed will help ensure you get there.

lesson 1: understanding values

If everything is important, nothing is. Below you'll find a list of twenty-five values. While most (if not all!) of them are values you'd like to model and instill in your children, circle your top five. After you have chosen five, select just three top priorities. If you're doing this exercise with your spouse or partner, work on it separately and compare your answers.

Love

Hope (Optimism)

Compassion (Caring)

Forgiveness (Letting Go)

Faith (Trust)

Generosity (Sharing)

Humility (Modesty)

Service (Helping)

Integrity (Honesty)

Gratitude (Thankfulness)

Patience (Waiting)

Courage (Bravery)

Wisdom (Understanding)

Peace (Calmness)

Inclusivity (Welcoming)

Unity (Togetherness)

Joy (Happiness)

Social Justice (Fairness)

Empathy (Understanding Feelings)

Environmental Stewardship (Taking Care of Nature)

Selflessness (Thinking of Others)

Responsibility (Doing Chores)

Encouragement (Cheering Others)

Holiness (Being Good)

Respect (Kindness)

My Top 3 Values:

Group Questions

1. How did you find the beliefs and values exercise? What stood out to you?
2. Imagine your children as adults, living out the values you have instilled in them. How do you hope they impact the world around them? How do their values impact their actions and choices?
3. How will your "top two" be modeled in your home?
4. What is the relationship between beliefs and values?
5. Micah 6:8 provides a useful framework and direction for raising a family in faith. Does it encompass everything you'd like to guide your family or is there something missing?

Building Faith Practice at Home

Remember: Your homework for each week is to do one of the faith practices in *Faithful Families: Creating Sacred Moments at Home*. The practices we encourage are found on the following pages of *Faithful Families.*

- Nighttime Blessing — p. 14
- Photo Prayers — p. 142
- Nature Prayer Walk — p. 152
- Counting the Days God Has Given — p. 16
- Gratitude Cafe — p. 18
- Choose Your Own — You're always welcome to choose one of the practices from *Faithful Families.*

Repetition is important! Try to do at least one of the practices two times.

After each practice, fill out one of the pages in your faith practice at-home journal, beginning on page 71.

Closing Ritual and Prayer

Give the group sixty seconds in silence to offer up prayers, recall the concerns brought up during the opening sharing time or in the discussion, and take a deep breath. After the minute of silence, conclude:

Leader: As we depart may we go with gratitude for all God has given us today and every day. May we trust in God to guide us in the journey ahead.

People: May the Spirit of Christ who has moved among us, now live within us. Amen.

LESSON TWO

Committing to the Journey

Objective

Parents and caregivers will consider the competing values in their time and attention and commit to making faith-at-home practice a priority.

The Symbol

Keys are a symbol of great responsibility. Keys to the house. Keys to the car. In this lesson, we'll focus on putting a symbolic "key to our family faith development" on our keychain.

60-Second Update

Opening Candle Prayer

Leader: God, we know that life calls us in many different directions. Be with us as we consider what truly matters to us.

All: May the Spirit of Christ who lives within us, now move among us. Amen.

(Candle is lit.)

Storytelling

Tell a story about a life decision you made that had bigger consequences than you thought it would.

Wisdom from Scripture

Joshua 24:14 (NRSV): "Now if you are unwilling to serve the LORD, choose this day whom you will serve, whether the gods your ancestors served in the region beyond the River or the gods of the Amorites in whose land you are living, but as for me and my household, we will serve the LORD."

Application of Scripture to Life

In Joshua chapter twenty-four, Joshua reaches a decision point. After all the battles, trials, and stories contained within the book, it comes time to affirm Joshua's commitment to God. And not just him, but all of God's people. Joshua makes the compelling plea we read about in chapter twenty-four: "If you're unwilling to serve the Lord, choose this day whom you will serve... but as for me and my household, we will serve the Lord." (Joshua 24:4)

Last week we made a conscious decision to identify which values are most important to us and which theological beliefs we most wish to have to guide us in our family life. Today we'll commit to putting the practice of faith at home in the forefront of life by saying, in a real and practical way, "As for me and my household, we will serve the Lord."

Perhaps you've seen this exercise: Imagine you have a jar, and in the jar, you're to put some big rocks, some smaller rocks, and some sand. If you put in the sand first, followed by the smaller rocks, there's no room for the big rocks. Put in the big rocks first, then the smaller rocks, and finally the sand and there's a different sense of organization. Not only does everything fit, but it's all in its proper place.

There are often circumstances in life we can't control (we'll be talking much more about this in lesson six), but to a large extent, we *can* choose what to prioritize and which rocks we'll make the "big rocks" in our life. The *Faithful Families* approach ensures that the values and beliefs we identified in the first lesson become the "big rocks" in our jar. That doesn't mean you have to spend hours every day on prayer and Bible reading. But it does mean committing to pursuing your values consistently and faithfully over and against other things. Raising children with the faith and values you want for them isn't the sand that squeezes in around the rocks in the jar. It's one of the big rocks.

lesson 2: big rocks exercise

Take a few minutes to identify which priorities in your life can be most clearly represented by the big rocks in your jar. Label the smaller ones as well, if you want. You can even add pebble-sized priorities or sand around the rocks as well.

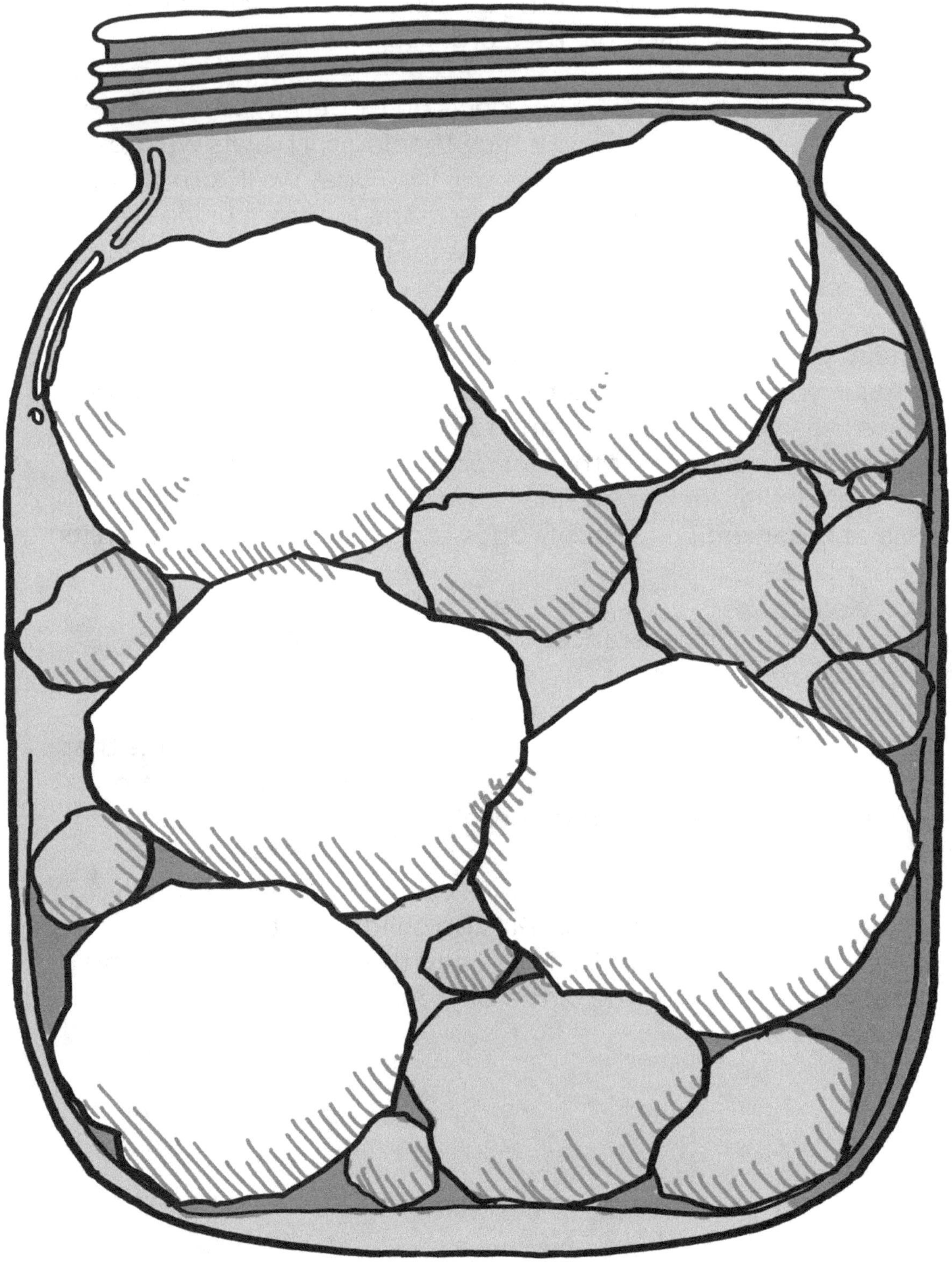

Group Questions

1. How did your priorities exercise go? What made it so?
2. What are the most important things ("big rocks") in your life?
3. What are some of the smaller rocks you need to fit around it?
4. Have your big rocks shifted or changed over time?

Building Faith Practice at Home

Remember: Your homework for each week is to do one of the faith practices in *Faithful Families: Creating Sacred Moments at Home*. The practices we encourage are found on the following pages of *Faithful Families.*

- Nighttime Blessing — p. 14
- Photo Prayers — p. 142
- Nature Prayer Walk — p. 152
- Counting the Days God Has Given — p. 16
- Gratitude Cafe — p. 18
- Choose Your Own — You're always welcome to choose one of the practices from *Faithful Families.*

Repetition is important! Try to do at least one of the practices two times. After each practice, fill out one of the pages in your faith practice at-home journal, beginning on page 71.

Closing Ritual and Prayer

Give the group sixty seconds in silence to offer up prayers, recall the concerns brought up during the opening sharing time or in the discussion, and take a deep breath. After the minute of silence, conclude:

Leader: As we go from this place, may we seal our commitment to the journey ahead, trusting God to guide us.

People: May the Spirit of Christ who has moved among us, now live within us. Amen.

Leader blows out the candle.

LESSON THREE

Finding Time

Objective

Parents and caregivers will consider when they have time for faith practice at home and plan for their own personal and family faith practices.

The Symbol

The clock measures where we are at any point in the day. What time is it? As we consider how we'd like to spend our time on what is most important to us, the clock is one way to keep us honest about our priorities.

60-Second Update

Opening Candle Prayer

Leader: Thank you, God, for the beauty and rhythm of time. Help us as we reflect on the time you have given us and be near as we dedicate it to your use.

All: May the Spirit of Christ who lives within us, now move among us. Amen.

(light the candle)

Storytelling

Tell about a personal or family routine that brings comfort, peace, joy, or structure to your life.

Wisdom From Scripture

Deuteronomy 6:6-7 (NRSV): "These commandments that I give you today are to be on your hearts. Impress them on your children. Talk about them when you sit at home and when you walk along the road, when you lie down and when you get up."

Application of Scripture to Life

Time has a way of getting away from us, doesn't it? Even when our lives are full of things with more meaning or value than endless scrolling, time flies. Those books we wanted to read. Those photos we wanted to have enlarged. That friend we've been meaning to have lunch with. What are some things you tell yourself you'd do if you had more time? Why aren't you doing them now? There are many reasons for this, but one is that we don't find (or make) the time and follow through. It's a simple (and yet so elusive) remedy: a schedule.

Experts in child development and parenting often emphasize the importance of routine and structure for children, particularly young ones (although routine and structure are very important for older children, as well). There is something cozy and comforting about a routine. You know what's coming. You don't have to think about it. For grownups, schedules and routines can cut out the decision fatigue that happens when there are too many choices to make. When do I load and unload the dishwasher? Every morning, rain or shine, just like brushing my teeth. When do I exercise, pray, or connect with God? In the morning every day, or during lunch three times a week? If we don't schedule these essential things into our routines, they won't happen. It's as simple as that. If we wait for enough time to take a leisurely walk or have a long conversation with a friend, we never will. We must put it on the calendar and fiercely protect the time, and then we must do it again and again, and again.

Last session, we identified the values and beliefs that are most important to us. This week we'll consider when, during a normal week, we have set aside time to practice these values.

Author Annie Dillard says, "How we spend our days is, of course, how we spend our lives. What we do with this hour, and that one, is what we are doing. A schedule defends from chaos and whim. It is a net for catching days. It is a scaffolding on which a worker can stand and labor with both hands at sections of time. A schedule is a mock-up of reason and order—willed, faked, and so brought into being; it is a peace and a haven set into the wreck of time; it is a lifeboat on which you find yourself, decades later, still living."[1]

I love the word *scaffolding* in that quote. Scaffolding is like a skeleton. It's a solid foundation. Dillard says that the *schedule* provides that structure, the routine.

Throughout these lessons, we're working to incorporate some faith practices into our routines. *When* we do these faith practices makes all the difference. We must put them into a schedule and stick with it. This isn't an easy solution. It requires great discipline and follow-through. To truly make it work, you'll need a lot of tools, including a strong community, but the following exercise will get you started.

---

[1] https://www.themarginalian.org/2013/06/07/annie-dillard-the-writing-life-1/

lesson 3: scaffolding/nets

"How we spend our days is, of course, how we spend our lives. What we do with this hour, and that one, is what we are doing. A schedule defends from chaos and whim. It is a net for catching days. It is a scaffolding on which a worker can stand and labor with both hands at sections of time. A schedule is a mock-up of reason and order —willed, faked, and so brought into being; it is a peace and a haven set into the wreck of time; it is a lifeboat on which you find yourself, decades later, still living."

— Annie Dillard

Take a moment to think deeply about these two questions and write your answers here:

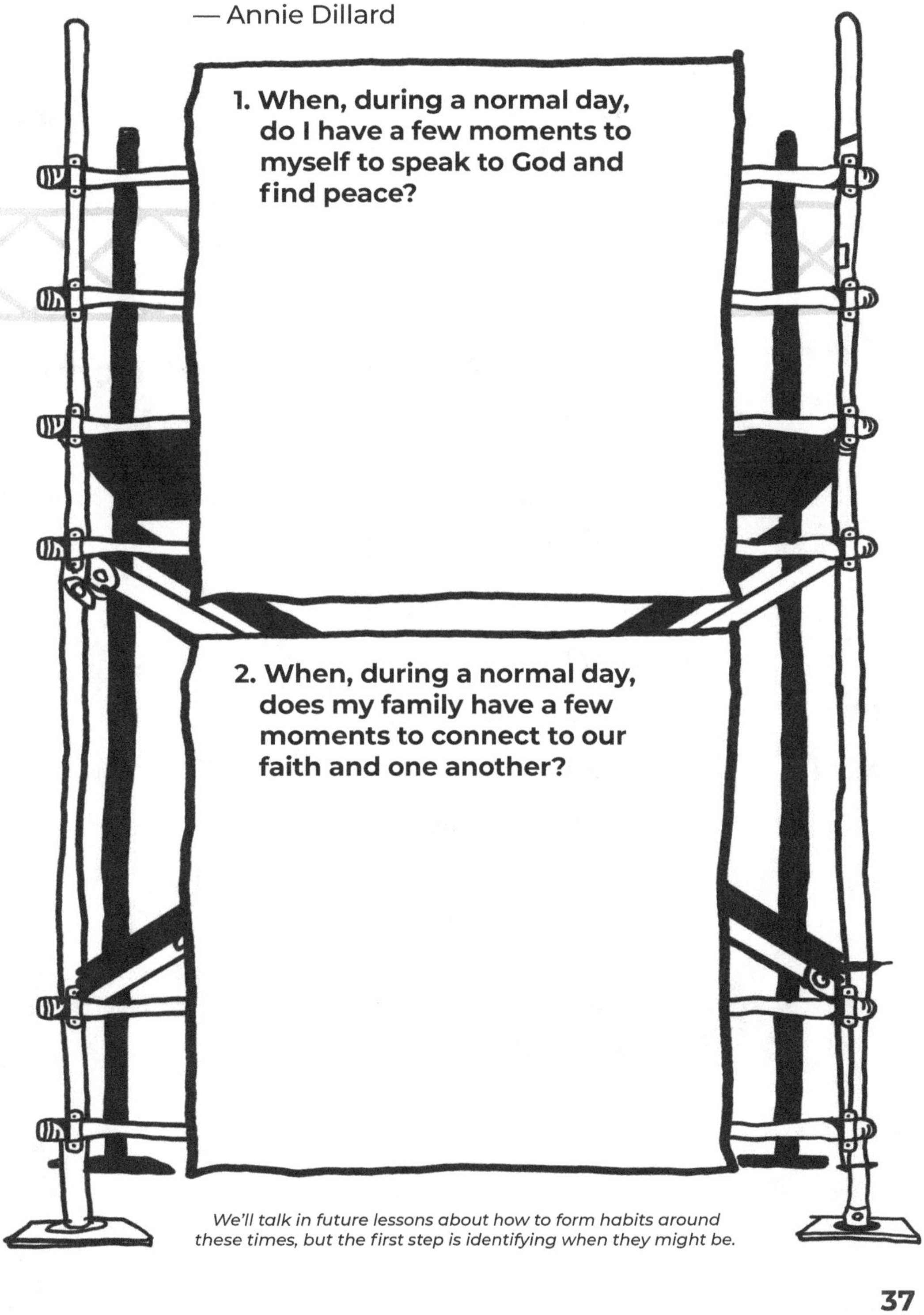

1. When, during a normal day, do I have a few moments to myself to speak to God and find peace?

2. When, during a normal day, does my family have a few moments to connect to our faith and one another?

We'll talk in future lessons about how to form habits around these times, but the first step is identifying when they might be.

Group Questions

1. What thoughts or feelings does the quote, "How we spend our days is how we spend our lives" bring up in you?
2. How does Deuteronomy 6:8 help you think about routine?
3. What is the difference between rhythms and routines that are constrictive, boring, and stale and those that are liberating, comforting, and holy?
4. Which activities do you find yourself doing daily, if not every day?
5. Which daily activities lend themselves, naturally, to incorporating faith practice?
6. How was your experience with your faith practice in the past two weeks? What surprised you? What frustrated you? What would you like to try this week?

Building Faith Practice at Home

Remember: Your homework for each week is to do one of the faith practices in *Faithful Families: Creating Sacred Moments at Home*. The practices we encourage are found on the following pages of *Faithful Families.*

- Nighttime Blessing — p. 14
- Photo Prayers — p. 142
- Nature Prayer Walk — p. 152
- Counting the Days God Has Given — p. 16
- Gratitude Cafe — p. 18
- Choose Your Own — You're always welcome to choose one of the practices from *Faithful Families.*

Repetition is important! Try to do at least one of the practices two times. After each practice, fill out one of the pages in your faith practice at-home journal, beginning on page 71.

Closing Ritual and Prayer

Give the group sixty seconds in silence to offer up prayers, recall the concerns brought up during the opening sharing time or in the discussion, and take a deep breath. After the minute of silence, conclude:

Leader: As we go from this place, may we be encouraged to make the time for the things that matter most.

People: May the Spirit of Christ who has moved among us, now live within us. Amen.

Leader blows out the candle.

LESSON FOUR

Establishing a Habit

Objective

Parents will understand the importance of repetition for habit formation and will consider how to establish a faith practice through repetition.

The Symbol

It's one thing to set aside time for something occasionally. It's quite another to do this over and over repeatedly. The calendar is the symbol of repeated action, whether daily or weekly.

60-Second Update

Opening Candle Prayer

Leader: All our days belong to you, O God, who created them and us with tender care and delight. Be with us as we consider what it means to establish habits that draw us nearer to you and to one another.

All: May the Spirit of Christ who lives within us, now move among us. Amen.

(light the candle)

Storytelling

Tell a story about a goal you achieved through repeated effort and practice.

Wisdom from Scripture

Philippians 3:12-14 (NRSV): "Not that I have already obtained this or have already reached the goal, but I press on to lay hold of that for which Christ has laid hold of me. Brothers and sisters, I do not consider that I have laid hold of it, but one thing I have laid hold of: forgetting what lies behind and straining forward to what lies ahead, I press on toward the goal, toward the prize of the heavenly call of God in Christ Jesus."

Application of Scripture to Life

In the book of Philippians, Paul talks about what it means to pursue a goal: forgetting what lies behind and *straining* toward what lies ahead. To get to the goal, he says, he must *press on*. This language suggests something challenging. Achieving important goals requires effort. Just because the faith practices we discuss in the *Faithful Families* approach are simple, doesn't mean it is easy to establish the practice. In addition to finding the time to practice faith at home, you must make that practice a habit, which is not easy to do. Remember Paul's words: "...press on toward the goal." Paul says that the prize is the "heavenly call of God in Christ Jesus." No words ring so true. Though establishing a faith habit is hard, the reward is great.

lesson 4: four laws, James Clear

Reflective Activity[1]: In his book, *Atomic Habits*, author James Clear gives four laws for building a new habit. The laws are:

1. Make it Obvious **2. Make it Attractive** **3. Make it Easy** **4. Make it Satisfying**

When it comes to building a habit of practicing faith formation at home, we can use the same four laws to help us on our journey to connect to God and our families through faith practice.

Law #1
Make it Obvious

In the last session, we talked about connecting our faith practice to a time in the day when we are already doing something together as a family; whether it's eating together, getting ready for bed, or taking a family walk.

What other ways might you make your faith practice at home obvious?

Law #2
Make it Attractive

How can you make your faith practice at home attractive? The ideas in *Faithful Families* try to do this for you, but the little luxuries you add to your practice can be uniquely yours.

Perhaps you'll snuggle under a special blanket for photo prayers or drink your favorite tea or coffee during Gratitude Cafe.

What would make faith practice at home attractive for you?

Law #3
Make it Easy

The easier a faith practice is, the better. Your practice doesn't need to be complicated or involved to be effective. A simple blessing or a few words of connection is all it takes. The benefit is the repetition and the consistency.

How could you simplify faith practice at home?

Law #4
Make it Satisfying

While it will be satisfying to answer questions in this toolkit, fill in a bubble in your habit tracker, or report back to your church community how it's going, there's a deeper satisfaction in seeing how family members draw closer to God and one another through faith practice. We hope you'll find it satisfying to fill out the form in the workbook to check off your practices as you complete them! Are there any other ways to make your faith practice satisfying?

1. The four laws of habit-building come from the book *Atomic Habits: An Easy & Proven Way to Build Good Habits & Break Bad Ones* by James Clear

Group Questions

1. How has your faith-at-home practice been going? What changes do you need to make to make it go even more smoothly?
2. How might you set your family up to succeed in forming faith habits by using the four laws discussed in the interactive section above?
3. So far, what have been the biggest challenges for your family in terms of establishing faith practices at home?
4. How do you think establishing a faith-at-home practice will ultimately benefit your family? How will it benefit you?

Building Faith Practice at Home

Remember: Your homework for each week is to do one of the faith practices in *Faithful Families: Creating Sacred Moments at Home*. The practices we encourage are found on the following pages of *Faithful Families.*

- Nighttime Blessing — p. 14
- Photo Prayers — p. 142
- Nature Prayer Walk — p. 152
- Counting the Days God Has Given — p. 16
- Gratitude Cafe — p. 18
- Choose Your Own — You're always welcome to choose one of the practices from *Faithful Families*.

Repetition is important! Try to do at least one of the practices two times. After each practice, fill out one of the pages in your faith practice at-home journal, beginning on page 71.

Closing Ritual and Prayer

Give the group sixty seconds in silence to offer up prayers, recall the concerns brought up during the opening sharing time or in the discussion, and take a deep breath. After the minute of silence, conclude:

Leader: As we go from this place may we press on toward the goal of forming faith habits that will last a lifetime.

People: May the Spirit of Christ who has moved among us, now live within us. Amen.

Leader blows out the candle.

LESSON FIVE

Enjoying Different Seasons

Objective

Parents will reflect on the different seasons of parenting and identify which stage they're in, which stage they've left, and which stage is next.

The Symbol

The camera reflects snapshots in time. Photographs are a great way to anchor us to the present moment. We can also look at photos from the past to help us remember the highlights of a previous era.

60-Second Update

Opening Candle Prayer

Leader: God of yesterday, today, and tomorrow, please be with us as we reflect on the many different seasons in our lives and how we learn through each one.

All: May the Spirit of Christ who lives within us, now move among us. Amen.

(light the candle)

Storytelling

Tell a story about your child's birth, baptism, or other significant milestone in their life so far.

Wisdom from Scripture

Ecclesiastes 3:1-8 (NRSV): "For everything there is a season and a time for every matter under heaven: a time to be born and a time to die;
a time to plant and a time to pluck up what is planted;
a time to kill and a time to heal;
a time to break down and a time to build up;
a time to weep and a time to laugh;
a time to mourn and a time to dance;
a time to throw away stones and a time to gather stones together;

a time to embrace and a time to refrain from embracing;
a time to seek and a time to lose;
a time to keep and a time to throw away;
a time to tear and a time to sew;
a time to keep silent and a time to speak;
a time to love and a time to hate;
a time for war and a time for peace."

Application of Scripture to Life

If Ecclesiastes were written about parenting, it might say, "a time for diapers and a time for potty training; a time for clinging to mama's knees and a time for pretending mama isn't needed at all; a time for strained peas and a time for an entire pizza." You get the point. Parenting is defined by different seasons and stages, and as we move through them, we find different challenges and joys along the way.

Though there's variation in how we divide the stages, childhood can be thought of in roughly the following stages:

- Infancy
- Toddler
- Early Childhood
- Middle Childhood
- Adolescence

One could even tack on a stage before infancy to discuss pregnancy and a stage after typical adolescence to discuss young adulthood.

As you look at this timeline, where do you find yourself on your parenting journey? Perhaps you are far along with one child and a little earlier on with another. Perhaps your child or children are just babies, and you see yourself looking forward to a long road ahead of you. Perhaps you're nearing the end of the journey and wondering where the time has gone.

Each stage has its joys and challenges. In the next activity, we'll take a moment to reflect on the stage you're in right now and to consider what you've just left behind and what is coming up soon.

lesson 5: snapshots

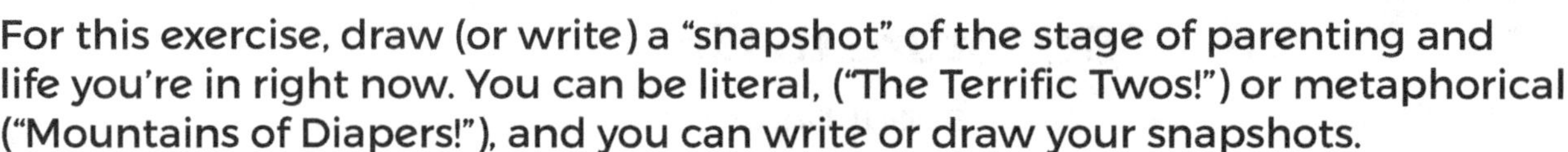

For this exercise, draw (or write) a "snapshot" of the stage of parenting and life you're in right now. You can be literal, ("The Terrific Twos!") or metaphorical ("Mountains of Diapers!"), and you can write or draw your snapshots.

A Snapshot of Before (What stage of parenting did you just leave?)

A Snapshot of This Present Moment (What stage of parenting are you in now?)

A Snapshot of the Future (What's coming up next?)

Group Questions

1. What is your favorite part about the stage of parenting you're in right now? Why?
2. What is your least favorite part about the stage of parenting you're in right now? Why?
3. What is coming up for you next on your parenting journey? How do you feel about it?
4. What did you just leave behind on your parenting journey? How do you feel about it?
5. Which stage of parenting seems to be the most challenging? The most fun? Which do you think your parents enjoyed the most?

Building Faith Practice at Home

Remember: Your homework for each week is to do one of the faith practices in *Faithful Families: Creating Sacred Moments at Home*. The practices we encourage are found on the following pages of *Faithful Families.*

- Nighttime Blessing — p. 14
- Photo Prayers — p. 142
- Nature Prayer Walk — p. 152
- Counting the Days God Has Given — p. 16
- Gratitude Cafe — p. 18
- Choose Your Own — You're always welcome to choose one of the practices from *Faithful Families.*

Repetition is important! Try to do at least one of the practices two times. After each practice, fill out one of the pages in your faith practice at-home journal, beginning on page 71.

Closing Prayer and Ritual

Give the group sixty seconds in silence to offer up prayers, recall the concerns brought up during the opening sharing time or in the discussion, and take a deep breath. After the minute of silence, conclude:

Leader: As we go from this place, may we be inspired to enjoy each season as we are in it, knowing that it may be fleeting.

People: May the Spirit of Christ who has moved among us, now live within us. Amen.

LESSON SIX

Integrating Difficult Moments

Objective

Parents and caregivers will reflect on God's presence in their lives through difficult moments and consider how to use these moments to help form their children in faith.

The Symbol

A candle is a symbol of the Spirit's presence. When we don't have the words to say, we can simply light a candle and be mindful of the Spirit. Keep one on hand as a reminder of God's presence when you need it most.

60-Second Update

Opening Candle Prayer

Leader: God, you are our refuge and strength in good times and bad. Help us this day as we consider how to parent in faith through the challenging moments of our lives.

All: May the Spirit of Christ who lives within us, now move among us. Amen.

Storytelling

Tell a story about a challenging time in your life and how you saw God at work through it.

Wisdom from Scripture

Psalm 46: 1-3 (NRSV): "God is our refuge and strength, a very present help in trouble. Therefore we will not fear, though the earth should change, though the mountains shake in the heart of the sea, though its waters roar and foam, though the mountains tremble with its tumult."

Application of Scripture to Life

When it comes to tragedy, grief, and hard times, the question is not *if* you will face them as a family, but *when*. Trials and difficult times are a part of life. Knowing this, and preparing for it, as a parent provides an opportunity to help form our children in faith. We can use hard times as stepping stones rather than stumbling blocks by helping our children learn that our faith is meaningful and available to us when we face trials of many kinds.

When it comes to natural disasters, we do this already. Whether it's some emergency food and water in the basement, along with a first-aid kit and bag with our secure documents or something more elaborate, most of us have some sort of emergency preparedness kit. This lesson is designed to help you think through a spiritual emergency preparedness kit so you'll know exactly what to do when the time comes.

In earlier generations, the defining news event of the time was the death of John F. Kennedy. For some, it was the *Challenger* explosion and then 9/11. For present-day children, perhaps it will be the COVID shutdown or something else. How do we help our children process these difficult world events? What about things like death, divorce, chronic illness, or other tragedies? How do we help our children through those, too? The following exercise will help you think through some things you might do when tough times come.

lesson 6: our spiritual-preparedness plan

Just as it makes sense to know the location of the exits before you take off on the plane, it also makes sense to think through how you'll handle tragedy and tough times with your family from a spiritual perspective.

Band-Aids and first-aid kits can heal the body, but candles and prayers heal the heart. In times of crisis, it's hard to think through what you'll do when trouble comes. This worksheet helps you think through some practical plans for family faith during difficult times.

Basic Items to Keep Around:

- ○ **A candle and matches**
- ○ **A favorite prayer or prayer book**
- ○ **A copy of *Faithful Families* or another book of spiritual practices (chapter 6 of *Faithful Families* contains practices for difficult times.)**
- ○ **Other:**

What can we do when trouble comes?

practice 1

Light a Candle

Whether it's a special candle only used in times of challenge or difficulty or an ordinary candle you have lying around, a candle prayer is a beautiful symbol of God's presence. Its light shines when the words won't come, and children will connect the need and the prayer. No need to worry about saying the "right" words, just pray for something simple that feels natural to you.

For example:

"We light this candle for _______ in the name of the Father, the Son, and the Holy Spirit, Amen." or "We light this candle for _______ with hope and love. Amen."

Add a picture, a printed news article, or a written prayer under the candle if desired.

practice 2

Flowers in the Water

This ritual is one to keep around for any representation. Perhaps it will be to honor the memory of someone who died, to let go of worry, to mark a new beginning, or to say goodbye. Get some flowers for this purpose, fresh or dried. Bring them to a stream, lake, or other body of water and take turns dropping them in the water. Afterward, say one of the prayers from *Faithful Families* or other words that mean something to you.

practice 3

Your Family Practice

Is there something special you'd like to identify ahead of time that your family might want to do in times of trouble or stress? Is there a special place you'd like to go or words you'd like to say? Think through what you'd like to include in this plan and write it here:

Group Questions

1. What was the defining traumatic news event of your childhood? Do you remember how you felt? What, if anything, did the adults around you say or do to help you process it?
2. What other challenging moments did you experience as a child, and how did your family or church help you through them?
3. What would you like to communicate to your children about God's presence in tragedy?
4. What would you say if your children were wrestling with how God could allow terrible things to happen? How might you express your personal difficulties in understanding this?

Building Faith at Home

Remember: Your homework for each week is to do one of the faith practices in *Faithful Families: Creating Sacred Moments at Home*. The practices we encourage are found on the following pages of *Faithful Families.*

- Nighttime Blessing — p. 14
- Photo Prayers — p. 142
- Nature Prayer Walk — p. 152
- Counting the Days God Has Given — p. 16
- Gratitude Cafe — p. 18
- Choose Your Own — You're always welcome to choose one of the practices from *Faithful Families.*

Repetition is important! Try to do at least one of the practices two times. After each practice, fill out one of the pages in your faith practice at-home journal, beginning on page 71.

Closing Prayer and Ritual

Give the group sixty seconds in silence to offer up prayers, recall the concerns brought up during the opening sharing time or in the discussion, and take a deep breath. After the minute of silence, conclude:

Leader: As we ponder God's mysterious ways, may we depart with hope.

People: *May the Spirit of Christ who has moved among us, now live within us. Amen.*

LESSON SEVEN

Creating a Community

Objective

Parents will consider the importance of supportive networks and communities and identify who is in their own networks.

Symbol

Perhaps a more obvious symbol of connection these days is the cell phone we use for texting and calling our friends. Yet, the postcard throws us back to a time when you'd get just a few lines from the people you love. A postcard takes a bit of effort—to write the postcard, get the stamp, and throw it in the mail—but the payoff makes it worth it.

60-Second Update

Opening Candle Prayer

Leader: Thank you, God, for the gift of one another. Hear our prayers, both spoken and unspoken, and be near to us in the next hour as we gather and share.

All: May the Spirit of Christ who lives within us, now move among us. Amen.

Storytelling

Talk about a time you reached out for help, even when it was uncomfortable to do so.

Wisdom from Scripture

Hebrews 10:24-26 (NRSV): "And let us consider how to provoke one another to love and good deeds, not neglecting to meet together, as is the habit of some, but encouraging one another, and all the more as you see the Day approaching."

Application of Scripture to Life

Relationship expert and psychotherapist Esther Perel said, "Let's talk about the new AI, artificial intimacy. We have 1,000 friends on social, but we don't have a single person who can feed our cat for us."[1] Ouch. So true. In many communities, it's truly hard to get to know one's neighbors. Technology has also made it easy for us to avoid one another or to be self-sufficient. We can go entire days without speaking to anyone if we so choose. At the same time, we're hyper-connected, always "plugged in."

Parenting is so much easier when we share the burdens and joys with others. We're not meant to go it alone, and yet so many of us do exactly that.

When asked to help a parent in need, most people feel grateful to be asked and jump at the chance to help. Hold a *baby*? Are you kidding? Where do I sign up! People love to be of assistance and feel trusted when brought into someone's inner circle to help. In a cruel twist, however, most people absolutely despise asking for help. Just the thought of reaching out to admit need is enough to induce a cold sweat or shaky knees. The result is that the parenting world is full of people who would be thrilled to help but are never asked.

The remedy is for somebody to go first and say, "I could use some help." Asking for help is a sure way to begin a friendship with another parent, particularly if it's followed by, "Happy to return the favor."

We need one another, and we need more than just digital "friends." We need a community.

---

[1] https://brenebrown.com/podcast/new-ai-artificial-intimacy/

lesson 7: reflective activity

My Community:

Building and nurturing a support network for your family is hard work, but it pays off. Take time to consider the different aspects of your support community including strengths and gaps.

If I needed help with an errand, childcare, or someone to pick something up for me, and Instacart/other professional services were unavailable, here are three people I would call who would help:

How I would feel about asking for help:

EXTREMELY UNCOMFORTABLE

FAIRLY UNCOMFORTABLE

PRETTY COMFORTABLE

EXTREMELY COMFORTABLE

Here's how I feel when someone asks me for help

EXTREMELY UNCOMFORTABLE

FAIRLY UNCOMFORTABLE

PRETTY COMFORTABLE

EXTREMELY COMFORTABLE

What are three things I could do to help build a local support network for myself?

Group Questions

1. Who do you turn to for help with parenting when things get rough?
2. Do you have more or less support in parenting than your parents had? Why do you think this might be?
3. In what ways does technology help you stay connected to other parents? In what ways does it hinder you?
4. How would you feel if a fellow parent reached out to you for help or support?
5. How does it feel to be the one reaching out to others for help or support?

Building Faith at Home

Remember: Your homework for each week is to do one of the faith practices in *Faithful Families: Creating Sacred Moments at Home*. The practices we encourage are found on the following pages of *Faithful Families.*

- Nighttime Blessing — p. 14
- Photo Prayers — p. 142
- Nature Prayer Walk — p. 152
- Counting the Days God Has Given — p. 16
- Gratitude Cafe — p. 18
- Choose Your Own — You're always welcome to choose one of the practices from *Faithful Families.*

Repetition is important! Try to do at least one of the practices two times. After each practice, fill out one of the pages in your faith practice at-home journal, beginning on page 71.

Closing Ritual and Prayer

Give the group sixty seconds in silence to offer up prayers, recall the concerns brought up during the opening sharing time or in the discussion, and take a deep breath. After the minute of silence, conclude:

Leader: Let us leave this space today knowing we are not alone and trusting in God to provide companions for the journey.

People: May the Spirit of Christ who has moved among us, now live within us. Amen.

LESSON EIGHT

Starting Before Ready

Objective

Parents will review everything they've learned in the past seven sessions and make a commitment to apply their learning going forward.

Symbol

A flashlight always comes in handy if you're stumbling around in the dark. Perhaps you don't feel equipped, yet, for the daunting task of raising children in faith, but take heart: you have all the tools you need!

60-Second Update

Opening Candle Prayer

Leader: God, we give you thanks for the gift of these past sessions together. Be with us once more as we reflect on the time.

All: May the Spirit of Christ who lives within us, now move among us. Amen.

(light the candle)

Storytelling

Tell a story about a time you worried about something that didn't come to pass.

Wisdom from Scripture

Matthew 6:33-34 (NRSV): "But seek first the kingdom of God and his righteousness, and all these things will be given to you as well. So do not worry about tomorrow, for tomorrow will bring worries of its own. Today's trouble is enough for today."

Application of Scripture to Life

"Today's trouble is enough for today!" That's a whole word when it comes to parenting (and so many other things!). Worrying seems embedded into the DNA of parents. Worrying about swimming lessons while the child is in utero. Wondering how to afford college before kids even start pre-kindergarten. We can and should plan ahead, to be sure, but stewing in worry is not the way. Jesus gives clear reminders of this in Matthew chapter six when he asks the rhetorical question: "And which of you by worrying can add a single hour to your span of life?"

The remedy to worry is simple in theory and difficult in practice: "Seek first the kingdom of God and his righteousness and all of these things will be given to you as well."

The reminder for us as we move forward on this journey of forming faith at home with our kids is this: we have everything we need already! The journey won't be perfect. In fact, it's *guaranteed* to have its ups and downs. You will face them as they come.

This journey has been about identifying all the tools you will need in your toolkit going forward. Now, there's nothing left to do but start! Over the last seven sessions you've built a solid foundation of faith practice at home. You've got additional sheets for you to continue recording your practice. If it helps you, photocopy the last page and keep the practice going. If you get out of the habit, you can start it back up again. Keep in touch with your leader and with one another, and don't forget to enjoy the journey.

lesson 8: looking back

As you move forward into making faith habits a part of your everyday life, take a moment to review what you've learned in the last eight lessons.

What would you most like to remember?

The Compass: Understanding Values

The Keys: Making a Commitment

The Clock: Finding Time

The Calendar: Establishing a Habit

The Camera: Enjoying Different Seasons

The Candle: Integrating Difficult Moments

The Postcard: Creating a Community

Group Questions

1. Which lesson stood out to you the most from the last eight weeks?
2. How will you carry lessons learned from this class into your daily life?
3. What support do you need in order to make faith practice a habit?
4. Which faith practices are most meaningful to you and your family after the weeks of practice?

Building Faith at Home

Remember: Your homework for each week is to do one of the faith practices in *Faithful Families: Creating Sacred Moments at Home*. The practices we encourage are found on the following pages of *Faithful Families.*

- Nighttime Blessing — p. 14
- Photo Prayers — p. 142
- Nature Prayer Walk — p. 152
- Counting the Days God Has Given — p. 16
- Gratitude Cafe — p. 18
- Choose Your Own — You're always welcome to choose one of the practices from *Faithful Families*.

Repetition is important! Try to do at least one of the practices two times. After each practice, fill out one of the pages in your faith practice at-home journal, beginning on page 71.

Closing Ritual and Prayer

Give the group sixty seconds in silence to offer up prayers, recall the concerns brought up during the opening sharing time or in the discussion, and take a deep breath. After the minute of silence, conclude:

Leader: Thank you, O God, for the many lessons of this time together. May the tools we have gathered help us as we seek to grow closer to our families, to God and to one another, not only this day, but all our days as well. And for the last time, as a group, we say together:

People: May the Spirit of Christ who has moved among us, now live within us. Amen.

faith practice log

MM | DD | YY

Practice completed:

- O **Nighttime Blessing** (14)
- O **Counting the Days God has Given** (16)
- O **Gratitude Café** (18)
- O **Photo Prayers** (142)
- O **Nature Prayer Walk** (152)
- O **Other:**

Who participated?

____

____

____

____

____

____

Overall Impression of the practice:

KIDS

GROWNUPS

General impressions:

Memorable moments:

Did you modify it? If so, how?

Notes to remember for next time:

faith practice log

MM | DD | YY

Practice completed:

- O **Nighttime Blessing** (14)
- O **Counting the Days God has Given** (16)
- O **Gratitude Café** (18)
- O **Photo Prayers** (142)
- O **Nature Prayer Walk** (152)
- O **Other:**

Who participated?

____

____

____

____

____

____

Overall Impression of the practice:

KIDS

GROWNUPS

General impressions:

Memorable moments:

Did you modify it? If so, how?

Notes to remember for next time:

faith practice log

MM | DD | YY

Practice completed:

- O **Nighttime Blessing** (14)
- O **Counting the Days God has Given** (16)
- O **Gratitude Café** (18)
- O **Photo Prayers** (142)
- O **Nature Prayer Walk** (152)
- O **Other:**

Who participated?

____

____

____

____

____

____

Overall Impression of the practice:

KIDS

GROWNUPS

General impressions:

Memorable moments:

Did you modify it? If so, how?

Notes to remember for next time:

faith practice log

MM | DD | YY

Practice completed:

- O **Nighttime Blessing** (14)
- O **Counting the Days God has Given** (16)
- O **Gratitude Café** (18)
- O **Photo Prayers** (142)
- O **Nature Prayer Walk** (152)
- O **Other:**

Who participated?

____

____

____

____

____

____

Overall Impression of the practice:

KIDS

GROWNUPS

General impressions:

Memorable moments:

Did you modify it? If so, how?

Notes to remember for next time:

faith practice log

MM | DD | YY

Practice completed:

- O **Nighttime Blessing** (14)
- O **Counting the Days God has Given** (16)
- O **Gratitude Café** (18)
- O **Photo Prayers** (142)
- O **Nature Prayer Walk** (152)
- O **Other:**

Who participated?

____

____

____

____

____

____

Overall Impression of the practice:

KIDS

GROWNUPS

General impressions:

Memorable moments:

Did you modify it? If so, how?

Notes to remember for next time:

faith practice log

MM | DD | YY

Practice completed:

- O **Nighttime Blessing** (14)
- O **Counting the Days God has Given** (16)
- O **Gratitude Café** (18)
- O **Photo Prayers** (142)
- O **Nature Prayer Walk** (152)
- O **Other:**

Who participated?

____

____

____

____

____

____

Overall Impression of the practice:

KIDS

GROWNUPS

General impressions:

Memorable moments:

Did you modify it? If so, how?

Notes to remember for next time:

faith practice log

MM | DD | YY

Practice completed:

- O **Nighttime Blessing** (14)
- O **Counting the Days God has Given** (16)
- O **Gratitude Café** (18)
- O **Photo Prayers** (142)
- O **Nature Prayer Walk** (152)
- O **Other:**

Who participated?

____

____

____

____

____

____

Overall Impression of the practice:

KIDS

GROWNUPS

General impressions:

Memorable moments:

Did you modify it? If so, how?

Notes to remember for next time:

faith practice log

MM | DD | YY

Practice completed:

- O **Nighttime Blessing** (14)
- O **Counting the Days God has Given** (16)
- O **Gratitude Café** (18)
- O **Photo Prayers** (142)
- O **Nature Prayer Walk** (152)
- O **Other:**

Who participated?

____

____

____

____

____

____

Overall Impression of the practice:

KIDS

GROWNUPS

General impressions:

Memorable moments:

Did you modify it? If so, how?

Notes to remember for next time:

faith practice log

MM | DD | YY

Practice completed:

- O **Nighttime Blessing** (14)
- O **Counting the Days God has Given** (16)
- O **Gratitude Café** (18)
- O **Photo Prayers** (142)
- O **Nature Prayer Walk** (152)
- O **Other:**

Who participated?

____

____

____

____

____

____

Overall Impression of the practice:

KIDS

GROWNUPS

General impressions:

Memorable moments:

Did you modify it? If so, how?

Notes to remember for next time:

faith practice log

MM | DD | YY

Practice completed:

- O **Nighttime Blessing** (14)
- O **Counting the Days God has Given** (16)
- O **Gratitude Café** (18)
- O **Photo Prayers** (142)
- O **Nature Prayer Walk** (152)
- O **Other:**

Who participated?

____

____

____

____

____

____

Overall Impression of the practice:

KIDS

GROWNUPS

General impressions:

Memorable moments:

Did you modify it? If so, how?

Notes to remember for next time:

faith practice log

MM | DD | YY

Practice completed:

- O **Nighttime Blessing** (14)
- O **Counting the Days God has Given** (16)
- O **Gratitude Café** (18)
- O **Photo Prayers** (142)
- O **Nature Prayer Walk** (152)
- O **Other:**

Who participated?

____

____

____

____

____

____

Overall Impression of the practice:

KIDS

GROWNUPS

General impressions:

Memorable moments:

Did you modify it? If so, how?

Notes to remember for next time:

Congratulations

You've worked your way through the eight lessons of the *Faithful Families Toolkit*. In a sense, your journey to solid faith practices at home is just now beginning. Your challenge now is to keep your faith habits going as your family continues to practice faith at home. Use the tools you've collected over the past eight lessons. Refer to the lessons often. Most importantly, reach out to your church leadership and fellow group participants for ongoing support. May the God who loves you and created you bless you and your family as you continue forward in faith. Be blessed.
—Rev. Traci Smith, 2024

Acknowledgements

To Rev. Dr. David M. Csinos, Professor of Practical Theology at Atlantic School of Theology in Nova Scotia, Canada, and Research Director of Family Faith Every Day. For understanding, from the very beginning, what my work is about and what it's trying to accomplish, and for being an intellectual sparring partner ever since.

To the team at Chalice Media Group for all of your logistical and administrative support and for your commitment to publishing resources that help families grow closer to God and one another through faith practice. Thank you specifically to David Woodard,, Connie Wang, Serena Ruiz and especially Brad Lyons, President and Publisher.

To Paul Soupiset, whose flawless graphic design has lifted up *Faithful Families* for years now. You have built something that is much greater than the sum of its parts, and I can't thank you enough.

To Caryn Rivadeniera for expert developmental editing. I can not think of a better choice than you for so many reasons, not the least of which is your unabashed love of group study materials! Here's to even more inspired action (at Maharaja's, of course)!

To Jessicah Duckworth, and all the friends at Lilly Endowment Inc. for the vision and leadership you have shown through the Christian Parenting and Caregiving Initiative. It is humbling to imagine the ripple effect of this work for generations to come, to the glory of God.

To Maud Lyon, a true *anam cara,* for all of your support, both the tangible and intangible.

To Laura Alary, for being a sounding board early on, the entire cheerleading squad during my crisis of confidence, and — most especially – for being true, consistent, and unfailingly generous.

To Arianne Lehn, Jennifer Grant and Glenys Nellist: you are (individually and collectively) the very, very best.

To all my other unnamed beloveds: you know who you are and I am *certain* you feel my love and gratitude even when it's not spelled out.

My deepest gratitude is always reserved for my husband, Rev. Elias Cabarcas. You inspire me with your life, and I'm grateful to raise Clayton, Samuel, and Marina with you!. You are my sunshine.

To Mom and Dad: This one is dedicated to you.